Norwegian AMERICANS

SPIRIT
of America®

Norwegian AMERICANS

By Ann Heinrichs

Content Adviser: Heather A. Muir, Assistant Professor,
University of Wisconsin-Eau Claire,
Eau Claire, Wisconsin

The Child's World®
Chanhassen, Minnesota

7

Norwegian AMERICANS

Published in the United States of America by The Child's World®
PO Box 326 • Chanhassen, MN 55317-0326 • 800-599-READ • www.childsworld.com

Acknowledgments
The Child's World®: Mary Berendes, Publishing Director

Editorial Directions, Inc.: E. Russell Primm, Editorial Director; Pam Rosenberg, Line Editor; Katie Marsico, Assistant Editor; Matthew Messbarger, Editorial Assistant; Susan Hindman, Copy Editor; Susan Ashley, Proofreader; Julie Zaveloff, Chris Simms, and Peter Garnham, Fact Checkers; Tim Griffin/IndexServ, Indexer; Dawn Friedman, Photo Researcher; Linda S. Koutris, Photo Selector

The Design Lab: Kathleen Petelinsek, Art Direction; Kari Thornborough, Page Production

Photos
Cover/frontispiece: Ole I. Gjevre, Marie Gjerve, and Kari Erickson in Fairdale, ND, circa 1890's.

Cover photographs ©: North Dakota Institute for Regional Studies, North Dakota State University/ Fred Hulstrand Collection; Hollingsworth/Punchstock.

Interior photographs ©: Bettmann/Corbis: 9, 24; Corbis: 6 (Historical Picture Archive); 7 (Christie's Images), 11 (Chris Lisle), 13, 15, 22 (Bob Rowan; Progressive Image); Getty Images/ Hulton Archive: 17, 28; Getty Images/ Time Life Pictures: 18 (Francis Miller), 25 (Ed Clark), 27 (Julian Wasser); Hulton-Deutsch Collection/Corbis: 8, 19; Nord Hedmark og Hedemarken Lag/S. O. Erickson: 23;Vesterheim Museum: 10 (Sando Collection), 12, 16, 21.

Registration
The Child's World®, Spirit of America®, and their associated logos are the sole property and registered trademarks of The Child's World®.

Library of Congress Cataloging-in-Publication Data
Heinrichs, Ann.
  Norwegian Americans / by Ann Heinrichs.
    p. cm.— (Our cultural heritage)
  Includes index.
  Contents: The promise of America—Spreading across the land—Traditions that live on—Gifts to America.
  ISBN 1-59296-182-7 (lib. bdg. : alk. paper)
  1. Norwegian Americans—Juvenile literature. [1. Norwegian Americans.] I. Title. II. Series.
  E184.S2H45 2004
  973'.043982—dc22   2003018096

13   21   24

Contents

Chapter ONE

The Promise of America

New York City, shown here in the late 1800s, has been the port of entry for many generations of immigrants. Millions of people from all over the world come to the United States hoping for a better life.

"AT FOUR O'CLOCK WE SAW LAND. WE WERE THE very first of all the passengers to see it. I shall never be able to convey to you my thoughts and my feelings. To see land once again! With hopes of landing soon! Thankfulness to God over-whelmed me."

Gro Svendsen wrote this to her parents. She had left Norway for America in 1862. After three months at sea, she glimpsed the coast at last. She could hardly contain her joy. Now, she felt, her dreams of a new life would come true.

Through the years, about 800,000 other Norwegians made the same voyage. All were filled with hope for a better life in their new homeland. They worked hard to accomplish their dreams and make valuable contributions to America.

Norway is a country in northern Europe. It's one of the **Scandinavian** countries, along with Sweden and Denmark. Western Norway faces the North Atlantic and Arctic Oceans. High mountains run right up to the coast. Norway's jagged seacoast is lined with **fjords.**

Norway is a country in which the sea and the land unite to form Norway's most distinctive geographical feature—the fjords.

Interesting Fact

In the 2000 census, more than 4.5 million people in the United States claimed to have Norwegian ancestry. The population of Norway today is about 4.5 million. So there are about the same number of "Norwegians" living in the United States as in Norway!

The mountainous terrain of Norway is beautiful, but it doesn't provide a lot of good farmland.

Norway has a long **seafaring** tradition. Norwegian warriors called Vikings sailed the seas, raiding faraway islands and coasts. Along the way, they discovered lands that had been unknown to Europeans. The Vikings also helped develop the economy of trade and gained much knowledge about shipbuilding and navigation. Explorers such as Leif Eriksson made great voyages of discovery. Many old tales and legends tell of the adventures of the **Norsemen.**

In the 1800s, Norway was not an easy place to make a living. The rolling hills and flat plains in the east were good for farming. But there was not enough land to support all of the people who wished to farm. Many farm children left for the cities, where they hoped to make a living, and

LEIF ERIKSSON WAS AN ADVENTUROUS YOUNG MAN. HE WAS MUCH LIKE HIS father—the Norse explorer Erik the Red. Erik taught Leif to be an expert sailor. As a teenager, Leif was already making explorations of his own.

Around the year 1000, Leif sailed westward to a faraway land. There he found rich pastures and abundant grapes. He called the place *Vinland,* meaning "wine land" or "pastureland."

Many historians believe Vinland was a spot now called L'Anse aux Meadows. It's in present-day Newfoundland, Canada. That would make Eriksson one of the first Europeans to reach North America. His voyage took place almost 500 years before Christopher Columbus arrived in 1492!

In 1964, President Lyndon Johnson declared October 9 to be Leif Eriksson Day. Why was October 9 chosen? Because on that day in 1825, the first Norwegian immigrant ship arrived in America.

▶ The California Gold Rush, which began in 1849, also drew Norwegian immigrants to the United States. When shipbuilder Christian Poulsen returned to Norway with a small fortune shortly after gold was discovered, the thought of treasure lured several of his countrymen to America. Unfortunately, Poulsen was luckier than most, since he had been present at the beginning of the gold rush. By the time many eager Norwegians made their way to California, it was harder to become rich so quickly.

Hok Hallengdal in Norway was a typical crowded farm village. Many Norwegians came to America because it offered open space for farming.

eventually moved on to the United States and Canada. In Norway's mountainous west, many people made their living as sailors, fishermen, or loggers. Shipbuilding was also an important industry.

Norwegians traveled to America for many reasons. Norway's population grew fast in the 1800s. Between 1800 and 1900, it more than doubled. As the population grew, it became harder for farmers to make a living. Norway was running out of good farmland. But America offered the promise of wide-open spaces for farming. It also offered job opportunities in its factories. Often, family members, friends, and neighbors came to the United States to be near those who had already settled there.

For some Norwegians, Norway's class system was unpleasant and unfair. Many people thought they would find equality in America. One **immigrant**

The interior of a church used for worship by members of the Lutheran faith in Eidsborg, Norway. More than 80 percent of Norwegians are members of the Evangelical Lutheran church, the official church of Norway.

wrote, "Here there is no distinction between persons, but every honest person is respected equally, servants as well as masters, in their pursuit of success and happiness." Wages were also higher in the United States. A sailor, logger, or factory worker could make much more money in America.

Like immigrants from many other countries, some Norwegians left to find religious freedom. The Lutheran Church was Norway's official religion. Other groups sometimes faced **persecution.** Some were Lutherans who had broken away from the official church. Others were Quakers—members of the Society of Friends. People were free to practice their faith in America, though.

The promise of religious freedom was a powerful force. It led to the first Norwegian settlement in America.

Chapter Two

Spreading across the Land

Cleng Peerson was born Klein Pederson Hesthammer. He became known as the "father of Norwegian immigration." Peerson's hometown of Tysvaer takes part in an annual emigration festival to honor his legacy.

CLENG PEERSON WAS A QUAKER FROM NORWAY'S Stavanger region. He left for the United States in 1821. He hoped to find a place where Quakers could live in peace. Peerson returned with good news. America was a fertile land, and it promised religious freedom.

On July 4, 1825, the ship *Restauration* pulled out of Stavanger. Onboard were 52 Norwegian Quakers, full of hope for a new home. For more than three months, they sailed the Atlantic Ocean. At last they stepped ashore in New York City. This was the first organized **emigration** of Norwegians to America.

Many more ships would leave Norway for America. Over the next

150 years, more than 850,000 Norwegians migrated to the United States. Many had read the "America book." That was a guidebook by Ole Rynning. It gave step-by-step instructions on moving to America.

Rynning said people should leave in the early spring. Then they could plant and harvest crops before winter set in. For the voyage, they should bring food that wouldn't spoil. People spent months preparing for their journey. They worked all through the winter—making clothes, preparing meats, making chests and barrels to carry things, and selling possessions.

Norwegians called this wild rush of emigration America fever. Many towns saw hundreds of their citizens leave. Ministers preached against the fever.

Interesting Fact

Fifty-two people left Norway on the *Restauration*. But 53 passengers arrived in America. Mrs. Lars Larson gave birth to a baby girl during the voyage.

OLE RYNNING REACHED AMERICA IN 1837. THE NEXT YEAR, HE WROTE *True Account of America for the Information and Help of Peasant and Commoner.* People in Norway called it the America book. It was a real how-to book for Norwegians dreaming of a new life in America. Here, in English, is some of Rynning's advice:

▸ "The best time to leave Norway is . . . early in the spring. . . . In that way something can be raised even the first year."
▸ "Those who wish to emigrate to America ought to take with them bedclothes, and clothing of fur . . . a spinning wheel . . . silverware . . . tools . . . a good rifle . . ."
▸ "The provisions for the sea voyage should include . . . pork, dried meat, salted meat, dried herring, smoked herring, dried fish, butter, cheese, . . . flour, peas, cereals, potatoes, . . . coffee, tea, sugar, pots, pans, and kettles."
▸ "For purposes of cleanliness it is necessary to take (a) linen for change, (b) salt-water soap for washing, and (c) good fine combs."

Rynning explained both true and false ideas:

▸ "Two things about the sea voyage are very disagreeable; namely, seasickness and **tediousness.**"

▸ "A silly rumor was believed by many in Norway; namely, that those who wished to emigrate to America were taken to Turkey and sold as slaves. This rumor is absolutely groundless."

Of course, Rynning had high praises for life in America:

▸ "Every one can believe as he wishes and worship God in the manner which he believes to be right, but he must not persecute any one for holding another faith."

▸ "In this state I have not yet seen a beggar. The able-bodied man is in no danger of poverty or need."

▸ "Women are respected and honored far more than is the case among the common people in Norway."

They warned of sea monsters, wild animals, and a miserable life. But the warnings did no good. As one minister grumbled, "A spirit of restlessness took possession of all."

Peerson's Quaker group settled in Kendall, in northern New York State. But for most of these immigrants, Kendall was only a stopping place. They knew they could find acres of rich farmland in the Midwest. Again, Peerson headed west in search of land. At last, he reached the fertile Fox River Valley in LaSalle County, Illinois. Its rolling prairies would make good farmland. Here, in 1834, Peerson established the first permanent Norwegian settlement in the United States.

From Illinois, Norwegians moved into Wisconsin and set up several communities. By the 1840s, Wisconsin was the main Norwegian settlement in America. Soon, however, settlers in both Illinois and Wisconsin faced a familiar problem—not enough farmland.

One group left for Texas in the 1840s. Norwegians would make settlements in Bosque County and other regions. Some Norwegians joined the California Gold Rush after 1849. Still others made the long trek to the Pacific Northwest—Oregon or Washington State. The snowcapped peaks

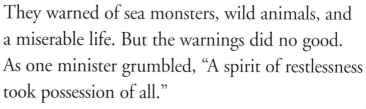

America has always been a place where people have sought religious freedom. These Norwegian Americans were members of the Greenwood Lutheran Church community of Hilsboro, Wisconsin.

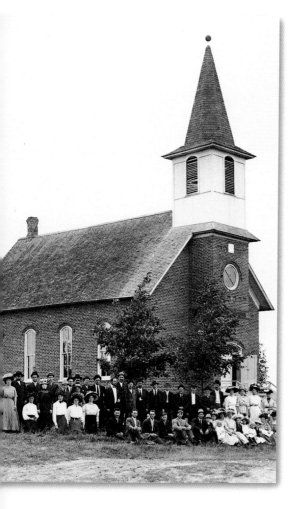

and rugged coast reminded them of Norway. Norwegian fishermen could continue their way of life there.

Many immigrants moved to Minnesota. First, they settled in the southeast. The town of Spring Grove became a completely Norwegian town. By the 1870s, Minnesota's Red River Valley had the state's biggest Norwegian settlement. Other newcomers moved to Duluth and other cities in far-northern Minnesota. They worked in iron mines or fished in Lake Superior.

Other Norwegians moved into Iowa, settling in the Decorah area. **Scouts** had told them glorious tales of Iowa: "There are smooth, sunlit hills . . . and rich, juicy meadows. . . . There is good water and sheltering woods along all water courses. It is surely a land which . . . flows with milk and honey."

Many settlers found new homes through the 1862 Homestead Act. It offered free land to anyone who would build a house on it and farm it for five years. In 1879, new lands opened up for settlement

A train delivers equipment to a farm in Minnesota. Many Norwegian farmers settled in Minnesota's fertile Red River Valley.

Interesting Fact

About 50,000 Norwegians lived in Minnesota in 1870. Between 1870 and 1900, the number of Norwegians in Duluth rose from 242 to about 7,500.

Saint Olaf College was founded in 1874 to give young women and men a college education with a Lutheran perspective. In the true spirit of America, though, people of all faiths are welcome there.

in Dakota Territory. Hundreds of Norwegian farmers rushed in. Norwegians were the largest ethnic group in North Dakota until 1920.

Most Norwegian immigrants lived as farmers. They cleared the land and used strong oxen to pull their plows. Some families built log cabins. Sod houses were common shelters, too.

Farming in the Midwest could be difficult. The immigrants often faced harsh weather, diseases, and knee-deep mud. Some immigrants had trouble learning English. They missed the comfort of hearing their own language. In time, though, they established Norwegian newspapers, libraries, and cultural clubs.

Norwegians also built their own churches and schools. In 1874, Norwegian pioneers founded Saint Olaf College in Northfield, Minnesota. Norway's Lutheran faith split into several branches. Each group held its own church services. They all kept a Norwegian identity, however. They formed Norwegian singing societies, aid societies, bands, and theater groups.

Many immigrants wrote letters back home. In Norway, these letters were called America letters. The arrival of an America letter was an exciting event. Families, neighbors, and townspeople all gathered around to hear the news. Some letters were even published in newspapers. Of course, the America letters only spread America fever!

Life in America was not always easy. But Norwegians were hardworking and tough. For most, the hardships were worth the trouble. They knew if they worked hard, they could better their lives. A group of Norwegians in Wisconsin wrote this in the 1840s:

"We have no expectation of gaining riches; but we live under a liberal government in a fruitful land, where freedom and equality are the rule in religious as in civil matters, and where each one of us is at liberty to earn a living practically as he chooses. Such opportunities are more to be desired than riches. . . ."

Interesting Fact

Today, Saint Olaf College is **affiliated** with the Evangelical Lutheran Church in America. However, it welcomes students of all religions and ethnic backgrounds.

An elderly Norwegian couple stands outside their simple home in the early 1900s. Many immigrants worked hard and endured great hardship with the hope that, in the end, their struggle would bring them a better life.

19

Traditions That Live On

LIKE MANY IMMIGRANT GROUPS, NORWEGIANS blended into American life. Large Norwegian-American communities grew up in the Midwest. Others thrived in California and the Pacific Northwest. Many immigrants settled right in New York City, where they had first landed.

Today, Norwegian-American farmers still raise wheat in Iowa and North Dakota. Norwegian Americans still catch fish in the Pacific Northwest. And Norwegian-American carpenters still carve wood in Brooklyn, New York.

Many Norwegian Americans keep up their craft traditions. One popular folk art is rosemaling. That's the art of painting flowers and curly vines on dishes, furniture, and wooden boxes. Weaving cloth by hand on floor looms is another Norwegian craft. The handwoven rya—a thick, shaggy wool blanket—once kept many a Norwegian fisherman warm.

Living in a land of forests, Norwegians became experts in woodworking. Today, some people of Norwegian heritage still carry on this skill. They carve wooden spoons, bowls, boxes, and cabinets. Norwegian folk music and dance are valued traditions, too.

Christmas is a joyous holiday in Norwegian culture. People decorate their trees with beautiful handmade ornaments. One traditional ornament is the Christmas basket. It's made of red and green paper woven together in the shape of a heart. Inside are candies, fruits, and nuts. Other traditional ornaments are woven from straw. They include the Christmas elf, or *julenisse,* and the Christmas goat, or *julebukk.*

Many Norwegian Americans celebrate Christmas Eve with a lutefisk dinner. Lutefisk means **"lye** fish." It is dried cod soaked in lye. When it is time to eat the fish, it is thoroughly washed to get the lye out and then boiled. *Krumkake* is a delicious holiday dessert. It's a light, crisp, cone-shaped cookie. *Lefse* and *rømmegrøt* are traditional foods enjoyed any time of year. Lefse is a traditional Norwegian flatbread, made of potatoes and flour. Rømmegrøt is a porridge made of soured cream.

Today, North Dakota has one of America's largest populations of Norwegian Americans. Every October, the Norsk Høstfest—*høst* is Norwegian for

The Christmas tree has been a favorite custom of the Norwegians since the mid-1800s. Traditionally, it is decorated with hearts, Norwegian flags, straw ornaments and Christmas baskets.

A young girl in traditional Norwegian dress takes part in a festival in Alaska. Festivals celebrating Norwegian-American culture take place in many cities across the United States each year. They typically feature Norwegian folk music and folk dancing, a parade, and lots of great seafood.

"autumn"—takes place in Minot, North Dakota. It's one of the biggest Norwegian-American events in the country. People come to enjoy traditional foods, music, and art. Another big Norwegian-American celebration is Nordic Fest, held in Decorah, Iowa, on the last weekend in July.

The Bay Ridge section of Brooklyn, New York, is an old Norwegian community. Every year, its residents celebrate May 17—Syttende Mai or Norwegian Constitution Day. They stage a grand parade to Leif Erikson Park.

Many Norwegian Americans enjoy tracing their family histories. They hold family reunions and trade stories about their ancestors. They are proud to be American—and proud to be Norwegian, too. As one immigrant said, "I love America and Norway, though each in their own way."

IMMIGRANTS FROM ONE TOWN OR DISTRICT IN NORWAY OFTEN SETTLED NEAR one another in America. By the 1880s, however, these groups were splitting up. Many Norwegians were leaving their farms for city jobs in factories and offices. Naturally, they grew homesick for their local traditions.

To keep in touch, they formed *bygdelags*. These were clubs of Norwegian Americans from the same region. Immigrants from Valdres, Norway, formed the first bygdelag in 1899. Many others sprang up in the years to come. Today, dozens of bygdelags exist throughout the United States. They still bring together descendants of immigrants from specific regions.

The Sons of Norway is another Norwegian-American network. They sponsor projects to preserve Norwegian culture. That includes classes in language, cooking, and crafts.

Many Norwegian Americans learn about their past from the Norwegian-American Historical Association (NAHA). It collects valuable information about Norwegian immigrants in America. The NAHA is based at Saint Olaf College in Northfield, Minnesota.

Gifts to America

MOST AMERICANS DON'T REALIZE HOW MUCH Norwegians contributed to American life. But Norwegian Americans helped create the United States as we know it. They have enriched American government, business, entertainment, science, and sports.

The Norsemen of old were great sea explorers. Today, a Norwegian American is a famous space explorer—astronaut Sally Kirsten Ride. She was the

Sally Kirsten Ride was not only the first American woman ever to go into space but also the youngest American to do so. During her six days in space, Ride worked on many experiments and performed tests of the space shuttle's robotic arm.

first American woman in space. She made her historic flight aboard the space shuttle *Challenger* in 1983. In 2003, she was inducted into the Astronaut Hall of Fame.

The glamorous movie star Marilyn Monroe had a Norwegian father. Many other beloved actors have a Norwegian heritage. One is Renee Zellweger. She starred in *Chicago* and *Bridget Jones' Diary*. Another is Kevin Sorbo. He played Hercules in television's *Hercules: The Legendary Journeys* series. Fans of the classic television series *M*A*S*H* will recognize another actor whose father was Norwegian. Harry Morgan won an Emmy Award for his portrayal of Colonel Sherman Potter on the hit series.

Film legend Marilyn Monroe was born Norma Jean Mortenson in 1926.

Two Norwegian-American brothers became famous actors—James Arness and Peter Graves. Their family name was Aurness, and they were born in Minneapolis, Minnesota. Arness starred in television's *Gunsmoke* series as Marshall Matt Dillon. Graves starred in *Mission: Impossible* and many movies.

The Andrews Sisters—LaVerne, Maxene, and Patty—were a famous singing group in the 1940s.

The sisters, born in Minnesota, had a Norwegian mother. Their cheerful, upbeat songs helped Americans get through World War II (1939–1945). One of their biggest hits was "Boogie-Woogie Bugle Boy."

Actor James Cagney was one of Hollywood's "tough guys." Cagney was part Irish, but his grandfather was a Norwegian sea captain. Other Norwegian-American actors include Robert Mitchum, E. G. Marshall, and comedian Pat Paulsen.

Two Norwegian-American senators from Minnesota became vice presidents of the United States. Hubert Humphrey was President Lyndon Johnson's vice president. He also ran for president in 1968. Walter Mondale was vice president under Jimmy Carter (1977–1981) and he ran for president in 1984. Earl Warren was chief justice of the U.S. Supreme Court from 1953 to 1969. His father was a Norwegian immigrant in California.

Eliot Ness was the son of Norwegian immigrants in Chicago, Illinois. He grew up to be a legendary law-enforcement officer. Ness chased down criminals such as Al Capone in the 1920s. The TV show *The Untouchables* and a movie of the same name were based on his crime-busting life.

Arthur Andersen's Norwegian mother always told him, "Think straight, talk straight." Andersen followed her advice to succeed in business. He founded the Arthur Andersen accounting firm.

Conrad Hilton was the son of a Norwegian immigrant. He founded the Hilton Hotel chain.

Have you ever heard weather reporters talk about "warm fronts" and "cold fronts"? A Norwegian immigrant invented these terms. He was meteorologist Jakob Bjerknes. Bjerknes studied storms and how they move across oceans and land. His work led to today's computer-aided weather forecasting.

Did you ever ride in a little motorboat? Its motor is called an outboard motor. It hangs from the boat's rear into the water. Ole Evinrude invented that type of motor. When he was five, his family sailed from Norway to America. Ole spent most of the trip in the ship's engine room. His fascination with motors and machinery led to many inventions.

Thorstein Veblen was an **economist** in the early 1900s. He was fascinated with the way people try to rise to a higher class. Veblen wrote *The Theory of the Leisure Class.* In it, he used the term *conspicuous consumption.* That means making a big show of buying expensive things. People still use that term to describe flashy buying habits.

Dr. Jakob Bjerknes is considered a pioneer in weather forecasting. He became a professor and taught at UCLA. His father, Wilhelm, was also a meteorologist.

> "Babe" Didrikson Zaharias wasn't satisfied with just one sport. After her Olympic victories, she went on to become a golf champion.

Knute Rockne is considered one of the most talented football coaches of all time.

Ole Rølvaag wrote novels about Norwegian pioneers in America. He is best known for his set of three novels—*Giants in the Earth, Peder Victorius,* and *Their Father's God.* They show the pioneers' many struggles in their new land.

Many Norwegian Americans made their mark in the sports world. Knute Rockne came to America as a child. Now he's called the Father of College Football. He coached Notre Dame University's star football team from 1918 to 1931.

Placekicker Jan Stenerud was inducted into the Football Hall of Fame in 1991. Born in 1942, in Fetsund, Norway, he played for the Kansas City Chiefs, Green Bay Packers, and Minnesota Vikings.

Track-and-field star Mildred "Babe" Didrikson Zaharias was the daughter of Norwegian immigrants in Texas. She won two gold medals and one silver medal in the 1932 Olympic Games. Sonja Henie was another Olympic champ. She won three gold medals in ice skating. She went on to star in movies.

As you see, America would not be the same without Norwegian Americans. They shared their talents to make life better for us all.

825 The first large group of Norwegians leaves Norway for America.

834 The first permanent Norwegian settlement is established in the Fox River Valley in LaSalle County, Illinois.

838 Ole Rynning publishes *True Account of America for the Information and Help of Peasant and Commoner;* Norwegians use it as a guide for moving to America.

840s Wisconsin has the largest community of Norwegians in the United States; Norwegians begin settling in Iowa and Texas.

850s Norwegians begin settling in Minnesota.

862 Congress passes the Homestead Act.

870 About 50,000 Norwegians live in Minnesota.

874 Norwegians establish Saint Olaf College in Northfield, Minnesota.

1879 Norwegians join the land rush to Dakota Territory.

1895 The Sons of Norway organization is founded.

1899 Immigrants from Valdres, Norway, form the first bygdelag.

1925 Norwegian Americans celebrate the centennial, or 100th anniversary, of the first organized Norwegian emigration to America; the Norwegian-American Historical Association (NAHA) is founded in Northfield, Minnesota.

1964 President Lyndon Johnson declares October 9 Leif Eriksson Day.

1978 The first Norsk Høstfest takes place in Minot, North Dakota.

2000 In the U.S. Census, more than 4.5 million people claim Norwegian ancestry.

affiliated (uh-FIL-ee-ate-ed)
To be affiliated means to be closely connected to something. Saint Olaf College is affiliated with the Evangelical Lutheran Church in America.

economist (ee-KAHN-uh-mist)
An economist is a scientist who studies how people produce and consume things. Thorstein Veblen was a famous Norwegian-American economist.

emigration (ehm-uh-GRAY-shun)
Emigration is leaving one's home country. The first organized emigration of Norwegians to America was in 1825.

fjords (FYORDZ)
Fjords are narrow inlets of the sea that flow between high cliffs. Norway's seacoast is lined with many fjords.

immigrant (IHM-uh-gruhnt)
An immigrant is a resident of one country who came from another country. Every Norwegian immigrant hoped for a better life in America.

lye (LYE))
Lye is a chemical material used to make soap and to preserve food. Lutefisk, a traditional Norwegian food, is dried cod soaked in lye.

Norsemen (NORS-men)
The Norsemen were ancient Scandinavian people, such as those who once lived in present-day Norway. The explorer Leif Eriksson was a Norseman.

persecution (purr-suh-KYU-shun)
Persecution is mistreatment of those who have different beliefs. Some religious groups in Norway suffered persecution in the 1800s.

Scandinavian (skan-dih-NAY-vee-uhn)
Scandinavian countries are those on the Scandinavian peninsula—Norway and Sweden—and Denmark. Norwegians were among the many Scandinavian people who emigrated to America.

scouts (SKOWTS)
Scouts are people who explore a new land to gather information before settlers come in. Norwegian scouts explored Iowa and reported back to hopeful settlers.

seafaring (SEE-fair-ing)
Seafaring is travel by sea. Ancient Norwegians were experts at seafaring.

tediousness (TEE-dee-uhss-nes)
Tediousness is dullness or boredom. Ole Rynning's book warned that emigrants would suffer tediousness on their voyage to America.

Web Sites

Visit our homepage for lots of links about Norwegian Americans:
http://www.childsworld.com/links.html

Note to Parents, Teachers, and Librarians:
We routinely verify our Web links to make sure they're safe,
active sites—so encourage your readers to check them out!

Books

Burgan, Michael. *Leif Eriksson.* Chicago: Heinemann Library, 2002.

Hoobler, Dorothy, and Thomas Hoobler. *The Scandinavian American Family Album.* New York: Oxford University Press Children's Books, 1997.

Lurie, April. *Dancing in the Streets of Brooklyn.* New York: Delacorte Press, 2002.

Places to Visit or Contacts

Nordic Heritage Museum
For exhibits related to the people who emigrated to America from Nordic countries
3014 NW 67th Street
Seattle, WA 98117
206/789-5707

Vesterheim Norwegian-American Museum
For artifacts and photographs reflecting Norwegian immigrant life in America
523 West Water Street
Decorah, IA 52101
563/382-9681

Index

About the Author

ANN HEINRICHS GREW UP IN FORT SMITH, ARKANSAS, AND LIVES IN Chicago, Illinois. She is the author of more than 100 books for childre and young adults on Asian, African, and U.S. history and culture. Afte many years as a children's book editor, she enjoyed a successful career a an advertising copywriter. She has also written numerous newspaper, magazine, and encyclopedia articles.